Connected  Mathematics™

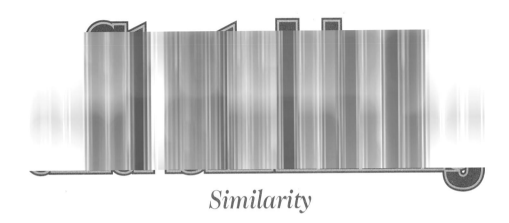

Similarity

Student Edition

Glenda Lappan
James T. Fey
William M. Fitzgerald
Susan N. Friel
Elizabeth Difanis Phillips

Prentice
Hall

Glenview, Illinois
Needham, Massachusetts
Upper Saddle River, New Jersey

Connected Mathematics™ was developed at Michigan State University with the support of National Science Foundation Grant No. MDR 9150217.

This project was supported, in part,
by the
National Science Foundation
Opinions expressed are those of the authors
and not necessarily those of the Foundation

The Michigan State University authors and administration have agreed that all MSU royalties arising from this publication will be devoted to purposes supported by the Department of Mathematics and the MSU Mathematics Education Enrichment Fund.

Photo Acknowledgements: 14 © Superstock, Inc.; 21 © Barbara Alper/Stock, Boston; 25 © G. Ricatto/Superstock, Inc.; 30 © Mark M. Boulton/Photo Researchers, Inc.; 37 © Nita Winter/The Image Works; 45 © Peter Menzel/Stock, Boston; 55 © J. Mahoney/The Image Works; 70 © Ira Kirschenbaum/Stock, Boston; 72 © N. Rowan/The Image Works

Turtle Math is a registered trademark of LCSI.

ISBN 0-13-053069-7
1 2 3 4 5 6 7 8 9 10   05 04 03 02 01

The Connected Mathematics Project Staff

Project Directors

James T. Fey
University of Maryland

William M. Fitzgerald
Michigan State University

Susan N. Friel
University of North Carolina at Chapel Hill

Technical Coordinator

Judith Martus Miller
Michigan State University

Curriculum Development Consultants

David Ben-Chaim
Weizmann Institute

Alex Friedlander
Weizmann Institute

Eleanor Geiger
University of Maryland

Jane Mitchell
University of North Carolina at Chapel Hill

Anthony D. Rickard
Alma College

Collaborating Teachers/Writers

Mary K. Bouck
Portland, Michigan

Jacqueline Stewart
Okemos, Michigan

Michigan State University

Jane M. Keiser
Indiana University

Angela S. Krebs
Michigan State University

James M. Larson
Michigan State University

Ronald Preston
Indiana University

Tat Ming Sze
Michigan State University

Sarah Theule-Lubienski
Michigan State University

Jeffrey J. Wanko
Michigan State University

Evaluation Team

Mark Hoover
Michigan State University

Diane V. Lambdin
Indiana University

Sandra K. Wilcox
Michigan State University

Judith S. Zawojewski
National-Louis University

Teacher/Assessment Team

Kathy Booth
Waverly, Michigan

Anita Clark
Marshall, Michigan

Julie Faulkner
Traverse City, Michigan

Chula Vista, California

Nancy McIntyre
Troy, Michigan

Mary Beth Schmitt
Traverse City, Michigan

Linda Walker
Tallahassee, Florida

Software Developer

Richard Burgis
East Lansing, Michigan

Development Center Directors

Nicholas Branca
San Diego State University

Dianne Briars
Pittsburgh Public Schools

Frances R. Curcio
New York University

Perry Lanier
Michigan State University

J. Michael Shaughnessy
Portland State University

Charles Vonder Embse
Central Michigan University

Special thanks to the students and teachers at these pilot schools!

Baker Demonstration School
Evanston, Illinois

Bertha Vos Elementary School
Traverse City, Michigan

Blair Elementary School
Traverse City, Michigan

Bloomfield Hills Middle School
Bloomfield Hills, Michigan

Brownell Elementary School
Flint, Michigan

Catlin Gabel School
Portland, Oregon

Cherry Knoll Elementary School
Traverse City, Michigan

Cobb Middle School
Tallahassee, Florida

Courtade Elementary School
Traverse City, Michigan

Duke School for Children
Durham, North Carolina

DeVeaux Junior High School
Toledo, Ohio

East Junior High School
Traverse City, Michigan

Eastern Elementary School
Traverse City, Michigan

Eastlake Elementary School
Chula Vista, California

Eastwood Elementary School
Sturgis, Michigan

Elizabeth City Middle School
Elizabeth City, North Carolina

Franklinton Elementary School
Franklinton, North Carolina

Frick International Studies Academy
Pittsburgh, Pennsylvania

Gundry Elementary School
Flint, Michigan

Hawkins Elementary School
Toledo, Ohio

Hilltop Middle School
Chula Vista, California

Holmes Middle School
Flint, Michigan

Interlochen Elementary School
Traverse City, Michigan

Los Altos Elementary School
San Diego, California

Louis Armstrong Middle School
East Elmhurst, New York

McTigue Junior High School
Toledo, Ohio

National City Middle School
National City, California

Norris Elementary School
Traverse City, Michigan

Northeast Middle School
Minneapolis, Minnesota

Oak Park Elementary School
Traverse City, Michigan

Old Mission Elementary School
Traverse City, Michigan

Old Orchard Elementary School
Toledo, Ohio

Portland Middle School
Portland, Michigan

Reizenstein Middle School
Pittsburgh, Pennsylvania

Sabin Elementary School
Traverse City, Michigan

Shepherd Middle School
Shepherd, Michigan

Sturgis Middle School
Sturgis, Michigan

Terrell Lane Middle School
Louisburg, North Carolina

Tierra del Sol Middle School
Lakeside, California

Traverse Heights Elementary School
Traverse City, Michigan

University Preparatory Academy
Seattle, Washington

Washington Middle School
Vista, California

Waverly East Intermediate School
Lansing, Michigan

Waverly Middle School
Lansing, Michigan

West Junior High School
Traverse City, Michigan

Willow Hill Elementary School
Traverse City, Michigan

Contents

Stretching and Shrinking

Many stores, particularly those that stay open late into the night, have surveillance cameras. One night the local Dusk to Dawn convenience store was robbed. The surveillance camera had taken several photographs during the robbery. By inspecting a picture of the robber standing in front of the cash register, police were able to determine the robber's height. How did they do it?

Draw a triangle on a sheet of paper. Can you divide the triangle into identical smaller triangles that are the same shape as the original triangle?

How tall is your school building? How high is the top of a basketball backboard? How can you find the height of something tall without measuring it?

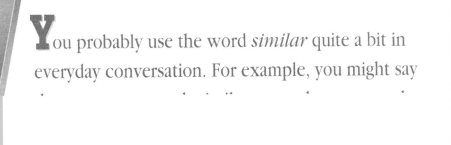

You probably use the word *similar* quite a bit in
everyday conversation. For example, you might say

Each of the shapes below has five sides
and five angles, but only shapes A and
C are mathematically similar. What do
you think it means for shapes to be
mathematically similar?

In this unit, you will learn what it means
for two figures to be similar, and you will
explore how ideas about similarity can
help you answer interesting questions
like those on the opposite page.

Mathematical Highlights

In *Stretching and Shrinking* you will explore the geometry concept of similarity. The unit should help you to:

● Recognize similar figures visually and identify that figures are similar by comparing sides and angles;

● Understand and use the equivalence of ratios of sides to examine similar figures and find unknown lengths;

● Understand the relationship between measures of lengths in figures and the scale factor relating two similar figures;

● Use the scale factor between figures to scale a figure up or down and to predict the lengths of corresponding edges and areas; and

● Use the concept of similarity to solve everyday problems.

As you work the problems in this unit, make it a habit to ask yourself questions about situations that involve similar figures: *What is the same and what is different about two similar figures? What determines whether two shapes are similar? When figures are similar, how are the lengths, areas, and scale factor related?*

Enlarging Figures

In this investigation, you will use rubber bands to make enlargements of drawings.
Although this is not a precise way to enlarge drawings, it's fun, and you can see

- When a figure is enlarged, which of its features remain the same?
- When a figure is enlarged, which of its features change?

1.1 Stretching a Figure

Michelle, Daphne, and Mukesh are the officers of their school's Mystery Book Club.
Mukesh designed a flyer inviting new members to attend the club's next meeting.

Daphne thought it would be a good idea to make a large poster announcing the meeting. She wanted to use the detective figure from the flyer, but at a larger size. Michelle showed her a clever way to enlarge the figure by using rubber bands.

Instructions for stretching a figure

1. Make a "two-band stretcher" by tying the ends of two identical rubber bands together. Bands about 3 inches long work well.

2. Tape the sheet with the picture you want to enlarge to your desk next to a blank sheet of paper. If you are right-handed, put the figure on the left. If you are left-handed, put it on the right.

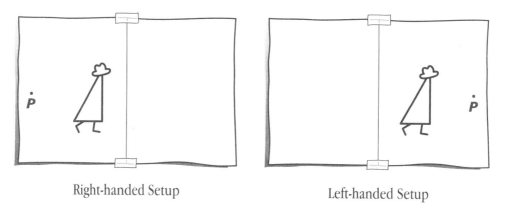

Right-handed Setup   Left-handed Setup

3. With your finger, hold down one end of the stretcher on point *P.* Point *P* is called the *anchor point.*

4. Put a pencil in the other end of the stretcher. Stretch the rubber bands with your pencil until the knot is on the outline of your picture.

5. Guide the knot around the original picture, while your pencil traces out a new picture. (Don't allow any slack in the rubber bands.) This new drawing is the **image** of the original drawing.

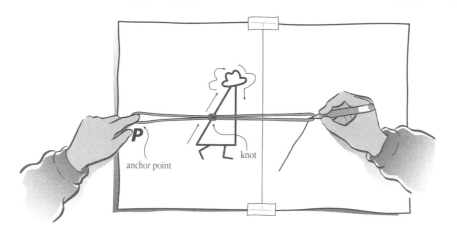

Problem 1.1

A. Use the method described on the previous page to enlarge the figures on Labsheets 1.1 and 1.2.

B. *Compare* is an important word in mathematics. When you **compare** two figures, you look at what is the *same* and what is *different* about them. Compare each original figure to the enlarged image you made. Make a detailed list about what is the same and what is different about them. Be

Explain each comparison you make in detail. For example, rather than just saying that two lengths are different, tell exactly which lengths you are comparing and explain how they differ.

Problem 1.1 Follow-Up

Michelle used her stretcher to enlarge triangle *ABC*. She labeled the vertices of the image *A'*, *B'*, and *C'* (read, "A prime, B prime, and C prime") to show that they *correspond* to the vertices *A*, *B*, and *C* of triangle *ABC*.

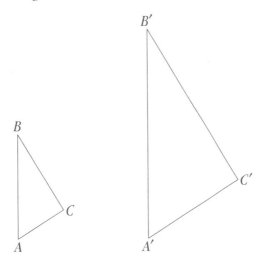

In mathematics, we use the word **corresponding** to describe how parts of a figure are related to parts of an enlargement or reduction of the figure. In the triangles above, ∠*BAC* and ∠*B'A'C'* are corresponding angles, and side *AB* and side *A'B'* are corresponding sides.

1. Name each pair of corresponding sides and each pair of corresponding angles in triangles *ABC* and *A′B′C′*.

2. **a.** Copy triangle *ABC* onto a sheet of paper. Choose an anchor point, and enlarge the triangle with your stretcher.

   b. Predict what would happen if you moved the anchor point up or down and further away from triangle *ABC* and then used your stretcher to enlarge it. Test your prediction by choosing a new anchor point and enlarging the triangle. Is your prediction correct?

   c. Predict what would happen if you moved the anchor point up or down and closer to triangle *ABC* and then used your stretcher to enlarge it. Test your prediction. Is it correct?

As you work on these ACE questions, use your calculator whenever you need it.

Applications

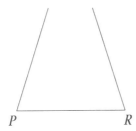

2. Copy square *WXYZ* and anchor point *P* onto a sheet of paper. Enlarge the square with your two-band stretcher. Label the image *W′X′Y′Z′* so that vertex *W′* corresponds to vertex *W*, vertex *X′* corresponds to vertex *X*, and so on.

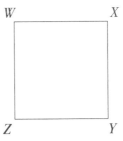

a. How does the length of side *W′X′* compare to the length of side *WX*?

b. How does the perimeter of square *WXYZ* compare to the perimeter of square *W′X′Y′Z′*?

c. How many copies of square *WXYZ* can fit inside square *W′X′Y′Z′*? (In other words, how do their areas compare?)

3. Copy parallelogram *ABCD* and anchor point *P* onto a sheet of paper. Enlarge the parallelogram with your two-band stretcher. Label the image *A′B′C′D′* so that vertex *A′* corresponds to vertex *A*, vertex *B′* corresponds to vertex *B*, and so on.

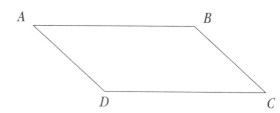

P

a. How do the side lengths of parallelogram *A′B′C′D′* compare to the side lengths of parallelogram *ABCD*?

b. How many copies of parallelogram *ABCD* can fit inside parallelogram *A′B′C′D′*? (In other words, how do their areas compare?)

Connections

4. Copy circle *C* and anchor point *P* onto a sheet of paper. Make an enlargement of the circle using your two-band stretcher.

P

a. How do the diameters of the circles compare?

b. How do the areas of the circles compare? Explain your reasoning.

Extensions

5. Circle A' is an enlargement of a smaller
circle A made by using a two-band stretcher.
~~Circle A is not shown.~~

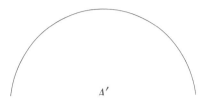

the large circle has a diameter of 16 centimeters. What is the combined area
of the two small circles?

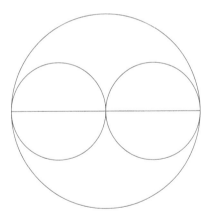

b. What is the area inside the large circle and above the two small circles?

7. Make a three-band stretcher by tying three identical rubber bands together. Use this stretcher to enlarge the drawing on Labsheet 1.1.

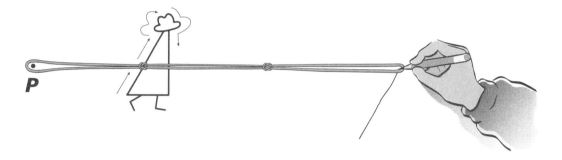

a. How does the shape of the image compare to the shape of the original figure?

b. How do the lengths of the line segments in the two figures compare?

c. How do the areas of the two figures compare?

Mathematical Reflections

In this investigation, you learned how to use a stretcher to enlarge figures. These

a. How would the side lengths of the enlarged rectangle compare to the side lengths of the original rectangle?

b. How would the perimeter of the enlarged rectangle compare to the perimeter of the original rectangle?

c. How would the area of the enlarged rectangle compare to the area of the original rectangle?

2 How does the location of the anchor point affect the image drawn with a stretcher?

Think about your answers to these questions, discuss your ideas with other students and your teacher, and then write a summary of your findings in your journal.

Similar Figures

Zack and Marta wanted to design a computer game that involved several animated characters. Marta asked her uncle Carlos, a programmer for a video game company, about computer animation. Carlos explained that the computer screen can be thought of as a grid made up of thousands of tiny points called *pixels.* To animate figures, you need to enter the coordinates of key points on the figure. The computer uses these points to draw the figure in different positions.

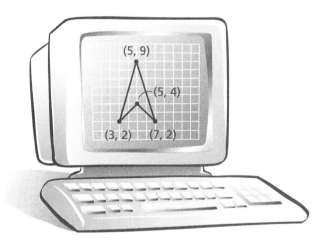

Marta told her uncle that sometimes the figures in their game would need to change size. Her uncle explained that a computer can make figures larger and smaller if you give it a rule for finding the key points in the new figure from key points in the original figure.

2.1 Drawing Wumps

Zack and Marta's computer game involves a family called the Wumps. The members of the Wump family are various sizes, but they all have the same shape. Mug Wump is the game's main character. By enlarging or reducing Mug, a player can transform him into other Wump family members.

Zack and Marta experimented on paper with enlarging and reducing figures on a coordinate grid. First, Zack drew Mug Wump on dot paper. Then, he labeled the key points from *A* to *Z* and from *AA* to *FF* and listed the coordinates for each point. Marta described the rules that would transform Mug into different sizes to create other members of the Wump family.

Lurking among the members of the Wump family are some impostors who, at first glance, look like the Wumps but are actually quite different.

A. Use the instructions below to draw Mug Wump on the dot paper grid on Labsheet 2.1B. Describe Mug's shape.

B. Use Labsheet 2.1A and two more copies of Labsheet 2.1B to make Bug, Lug, Thug, and Zug. After drawing the characters, compare them to Mug. Which characters are the impostors?

C. Compare Mug to the other characters. What things are the same about Mug and Zug? Mug and Lug? Mug and Bug? Mug and Thug? What things are different? Think about the general shape, the lengths of sides, and the angles of each figure.

Instructions for drawing Wumps

1. To draw Mug, use the sets of coordinate pairs given in the chart on the next page. Plot the points from the "Mug Wump" column on Labsheet 2.1B. Connect the points with line segments as follows:
   - For Set 1, connect the points in order, and then connect the last point to the first point.
   - For Set 2, connect the points in order (don't connect the last point to the first point).
   - For Set 3, connect the points in order, and then connect the last point to the first point.
   - For Set 4, make a dot at each point (don't connect the dots).

2. To draw Zug, Lug, Bug, and Thug, use the given rule to find the coordinates of each point. For example, the rule for finding the points for Zug is $(2x, 2y)$. This means that you multiply each of Mug's coordinates by 2. Point A on Mug is $(2, 0)$, so the corresponding point A on Zug is $(4, 0)$. Point B on Mug is $(2, 4)$, so the corresponding point B on Zug is $(4, 8)$.

3. Plot the points for Zug, Lug, Bug, and Thug, and connect them according to the directions in step 2.

Point	Mug Wump (x, y)	Zug (2x, 2y)	Lug (3x, y)	Bug (3x, 3y)	Thug (x, 3y)
Rule	(x, y)	(2x, 2y)	(3x, y)	(3x, 3y)	(x, 3y)
Point	**Set 1**	**Set 1**	**Set 1**	**Set 1**	**Set 1**
A	(2, 0)	(4, 0)			
B	(2, 4)	(4, 8)			
C	(0, 4)				
D	(0, 5)				
E	(2, 5)				
M	(7, 8)				
N	(5, 5)				
O	(7, 5)				
P	(7, 4)				
Q	(5, 4)				
R	(5, 0)				
S	(4, 0)				
T	(4, 3)				
U	(3, 3)				
V	(3, 0) (connect V to A)				
	Set 2 (start over)	**Set 2**	**Set 2**	**Set 2**	**Set 2**
W	(1, 8)				
X	(2, 7)				
Y	(5, 7)				
Z	(6, 8)				
	Set 3 (start over)	**Set 3**	**Set 3**	**Set 3**	**Set 3**
AA	(3, 8)				
BB	(4, 8)				
CC	(4, 10)				
DD	(3, 10) (connect DD to AA)				
	Set 4 (start over)	**Set 4**	**Set 4**	**Set 4**	**Set 4**
EE	(2, 11) (make a dot)				
FF	(5, 11) (make a dot)				

Problem 2.1 Follow-Up

1. In mathematics, we say that figures like Mug and Zug (but not Mug and Lug) are **similar.** What do you think it means for two figures to be mathematically similar?

2. The members of the Wump family are all similar. How do their corresponding sides compare? How do their corresponding angles compare?

2.2 Nosing Around

All the members of the Wump family have the same angle measures. Is having the same angle measures enough to make two figures similar? All rectangles have four right angles. Are all rectangles similar? What about these two rectangles?

These rectangles are not similar, because they don't have the same shape—one is tall and skinny, and the other looks like a square. To be similar, it is not enough for figures to have the same angle measures.

In this problem, you will investigate rectangles more closely to try to figure out what else is necessary for two rectangles to be similar. You will compare side lengths, angle measures, and perimeters.

One way to compare two quantities is to form a **ratio**. For example, Mug Wump's nose is 1 unit wide and 2 units long. To compare the width to the length, we can use the ratio *1 to 2*, which can also be written as the fraction $\frac{1}{2}$.

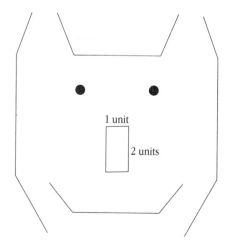

Problem 2.2

Copy the chart below. The Wumps in the chart are numbered according to their size. Mug is Wump 1. Since the segments that make up Zug are twice as long as the segments that make up Mug, Zug is Wump 2. Since the segments that make up Bug are three times as long as the segments that make up Mug, Bug is Wump 3. Since Lug and Thug are not similar to the Wumps, they are at the bottom of the chart.

C. The rule for making Wump 4 is $(4x, 4y)$. The rule for making Wump 5 is $(5x, 5y)$. Add data to the chart for Wumps 4 and 5. Do their noses fit the patterns you noticed in part B?

D. Use the patterns you found to add data for Wumps 10, 20, and 100 to the chart. Explain your reasoning.

E. Do Lug's nose and Thug's nose seem to fit the patterns you found for the Wumps? If not, what makes them different?

The Wump Noses (Plus Lug and Thug)

Wump	Width of nose	Length of nose	$\dfrac{\text{Width}}{\text{Length}}$	Perimeter
Wump 1 (Mug)	1	2	$\frac{1}{2}$	
Wump 2 (Zug)	2			
Wump 3 (Bug)	3			
Wump 4				
Wump 5				
⋮				
Wump 10				
Wump 20				
Wump 100				
Lug				
Thug				

■ Problem 2.2 Follow-Up

To find the length, width, and perimeter of Zug's nose, we can multiply the length, width, and perimeter of Mug's nose by 2. The number 2 is called the *scale factor* from Mug's nose to Zug's nose. The **scale factor** is the number that we multiply the dimensions of an original figure by to get the dimensions of an enlarged or reduced figure.

The scale factor from Mug to Bug is 3. You can multiply the side lengths of Mug's nose by 3 to find the side lengths of Bug's nose. We can also say that the side lengths and the perimeters *grow by a scale factor of 3.*

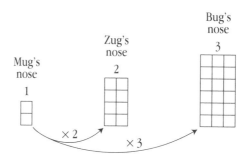

1. Is there a scale factor from Mug's nose to Wump 4's nose? Why or why not?

2. Is there a scale factor from Mug's nose to Thug's nose? Why or why not?

3. The dimensions of Bug's nose are 3 × 6. Suppose this nose is enlarged by a scale factor of 3.
   a. What are the dimensions of the new nose?
   b. What is the perimeter of the new nose?

4. a. What is the scale factor from Wump 2 to Wump 10?
   b. What is the scale factor from Wump 10 to Wump 2?

2.3 Making Wump Hats

Zack and Marta experimented with multiplying each of Mug's coordinates by different whole numbers to create other similar figures. Marta wondered how multiplying the coordinates by a decimal, or adding numbers to or subtracting numbers from each coordinate, would affect Mug's shape. When she asked her uncle about this, he gave her the coordinates for a new shape, a hat for Mug to wear, and some rules to try on

A	(0, 4)	(2, 0)	(5, 5)	(0, 0)	(0, 12)	(0, 2)
B	(0, 1)					
C	(6, 1)					
D	(4, 2)					
E	(4, 4)					
F	(3, 5)					
G	(1, 5)					
H	(0, 4)					

Problem 2.3

Use the table and dot paper grids on Labsheets 2.3A and 2.3B.

- To make Mug's hat, plot points *A–H* from the Hat 1 column on the grid labeled Hat 1, connecting the points as you go.

- For Hats 2–6, use the rules in the table to fill in the coordinates for each column. Then, plot each hat on the appropriate grid, connecting the points as you go.

■ Problem 2.3 Follow-Up

1. What rule would make a hat with line segments $\frac{1}{3}$ the length of Hat 1's line segments?

2. What happens to a figure on a coordinate grid when you add to or subtract from its coordinates?

3. What rule would make a hat the same size as Hat 1 but moved up 2 units on the grid?

4. What rule would make a hat with line segments twice as long as Hat 1's line segments and moved 8 units to the right?

As you work on these ACE questions, use your calculator whenever you need it.

Applications

1. The triangles below are similar.

   a. Name the pairs of corresponding sides.

   b. Name the pairs of corresponding angles.

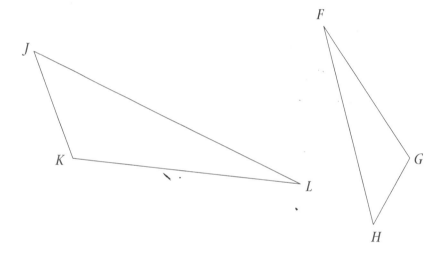

2. Mug's grandparents, Chug and Hug, are the fourth and fifth members of the Wump family (in the table for Problem 2.2, Chug is Wump 4 and Hug is Wump 5). How do the side lengths and angle measures of Mug's grandparents compare to the side lengths and angle measures of Mug? You may use the table from Problem 2.2 to help you answer this question.

3. If you used the rule $(6x, 6y)$ to transform Mug into a new figure, how would the angles of the new figure compare to Mug's angles? How would the side lengths of the new figure compare to Mug's side lengths?

4. If you used the rule $(0.5x, 0.5y)$ to transform Mug into a new figure, how would the angles of the new figure compare to Mug's angles? How would the side lengths of the new figure compare to Mug's side lengths?

5. If you used the rule $(3x + 1, 3y - 4)$ to transform Mug into a new figure, how would the angles of the new figure compare to Mug's angles? How would the side lengths of the new figure compare to Mug's side lengths? How would the location of the new figure compare to Mug's location?

measures of the corresponding angles of triangle *ABC?*

e. Are triangles *ABC* and $A'B'C'$ similar? Explain.

7. a. Draw a triangle *XYZ* with vertices *X* (5, 8), *Y* (0, 5), and *Z* (10, 2).

b. Apply a rule to triangle *XYZ* to get a similar triangle, $X'Y'Z'$, with a scale factor of 1. What rule did you use? How do the lengths of the sides of triangle $X'Y'Z'$ compare to the lengths of the corresponding sides of triangle *XYZ?*

c. Apply a rule to triangle *XYZ* to get a similar triangle, $X''Y''Z''$, with a scale factor of $\frac{1}{5}$. What rule did you use? How do the lengths of the sides of triangle $X''Y''Z''$ compare to the lengths of the corresponding sides of triangle *XYZ?*

8. a. Use triangle *ABC* from question 6 and the rule $(3x, y)$ to draw a new triangle.

b. How do the measures of the angles of the new triangle compare to the measures of the corresponding angles of triangle *ABC?*

c. Are the two triangles similar? Explain.

9. a. Copy rectangle *ABCD* onto a piece of grid paper.

b. Make a similar rectangle by applying a scale factor of 1.5 to rectangle *ABCD*. Label the new rectangle *A'B'C'D'*.

c. Make another similar rectangle by applying a scale factor of 0.25 to rectangle *ABCD*. Label the new rectangle *A"B"C"D"*.

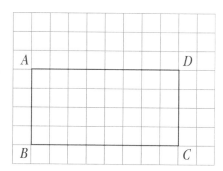

d. Tell how the lengths of the sides of each new rectangle compare to the lengths of the corresponding sides of rectangle *ABCD*.

e. Are rectangles *A'B'C'D'* and *A"B"C"D"* similar to each other? If so, what is the scale factor from rectangle *A'B'C'D'* to rectangle *A"B"C"D"*? What is the scale factor from rectangle *A"B"C"D"* to rectangle *A'B'C'D'*?

f. If you make a rectangle by adding 3 units to each side of rectangle *ABCD*, will it be similar to rectangle *ABCD*? Explain your reasoning.

10. Redraw Hat 1 (from Problem 2.3). Draw a new hat by applying the rule $(2x + 1, 2y + 2)$ to Hat 1. How does the new hat compare to Hat 1? Are they similar? Explain your reasoning.

Connections

11. a. On centimeter grid paper, draw a rectangle with an area of 14 square centimeters. Label it *ABCD*.

b. Use a rule to transform rectangle *ABCD* into a rectangle that is twice as long and twice as wide. Label the rectangle *A'B'C'D'*. What rule did you use to make rectangle *A'B'C'D'*?

c. What is the perimeter of rectangle *A'B'C'D'*? How does it compare to the perimeter of rectangle *ABCD*?

12. You can think of a map as a reduced
copy of a real country, state, or city. A
map is similar to the place it represents.
Below is a map of South Africa. The
scale for the map is 1 centimeter =

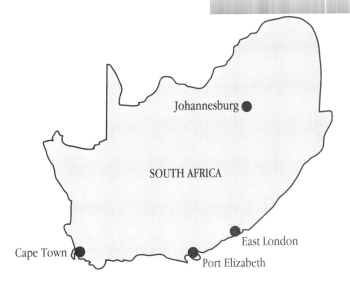

a. Cape Town to Port Elizabeth

b. Johannesburg to East London

Extensions

13. Select a drawing of a comic strip character from a newspaper or magazine. Draw a grid over the figure, or tape a transparent grid on top of the figure. Identify key points on the figure and then enlarge the figure by applying the rule $(2x, 2y)$ to the points.

14. Point A has coordinates $(2, 4)$, point B has coordinates $(6, 1)$, and point C has coordinates $(1, 1)$.

    a. A rule is appled to A, B, and C to get A', B', and C'. Point A' is at $(7, 3)$ and point B' is at $(11, 0)$. Where is point C' located?

    b. A different rule is applied to A, B, and C to get A'', B'', and C''. Point A'' is at $(4, 7)$ and point B'' is at $(12, 1)$. Where is point C'' located?

    c. A different rule is applied to A, B, and C to get A''', B''', and C'''. Point A''' is at $(6, 7)$ and point B''' is at $(10, 1)$. Where is point C''' located?

Mathematical Reflections

In this investigation, you made a character named Mug Wump on a coordinate

What types of rules produced figures similar to Mug Wump? What types of rules did not? Explain your answers.

3 If two figures are similar, describe the relationships between their

a. general shapes

b. angle measures

c. side lengths

Think about your answers to these questions, discuss your ideas with other students and your teacher, and then write a summary of your findings in your journal.

Patterns of Similar Figures

In the last investigation, you met the Wump family. You found that Mug, Bug, and Zug are similar—they have exactly the same shape. You also discovered that, to make a figure that is similar to a given figure, you keep the same angles and multiply each length of the original figure by the same number. For example, to go from Mug to Zug, you use the same angles and multiply each length by 2. To make a smaller member of the Wump family, you could shrink Mug by keeping the same angles and multiplying each length by a number less than 1, such as 0.5.

3.1 Identifying Similar Figures

How good are you at spotting changes in a figure's shape? Can you look at two figures and decide whether they are similar? In the last investigation, you learned some mathematical ideas about what makes figures similar. Here, you will use your visual perception to predict which figures might be similar, and then use mathematics to check your predictions.

Problem 3.1

Examine the four sets of polygons on Labsheet 3.1. Two shapes in each set are similar, and the other is an impostor.

In each set, which polygons are similar? Explain your answers. You may cut out the polygons if it helps you think about the question.

■ Problem 3.1 Follow-Up

1. For each pair of similar figures on Labsheet 3.1, tell what number the side lengths of the small figure must be multiplied by to get the side lengths of the large figure. (You learned that this number is the scale factor from the small figure to the large figure.)

2. For each pair of similar figures on Labsheet 3.1, tell what number the side lengths of the large figure must be multiplied by to get the side lengths of the small figure. (This number is the scale factor from the large figure to the small figure.)

3. How are the scale factors in parts 1 and 2 related?

Rectangle set

Parallelogram set

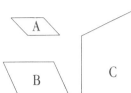

3.2 Building with Rep-tiles

A **rep-tile** is a shape whose copies can be put together to make a larger, similar shape. The small triangle below is a rep-tile. The two large triangles are formed from copies of this rep-tile. Can you explain why each large triangle is similar to the small triangle?

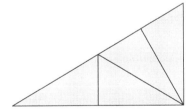
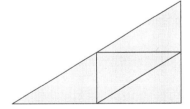

This reptile is *not* a rep-tile.

In this problem, your challenge is to figure out which of the shapes below are rep-tiles.

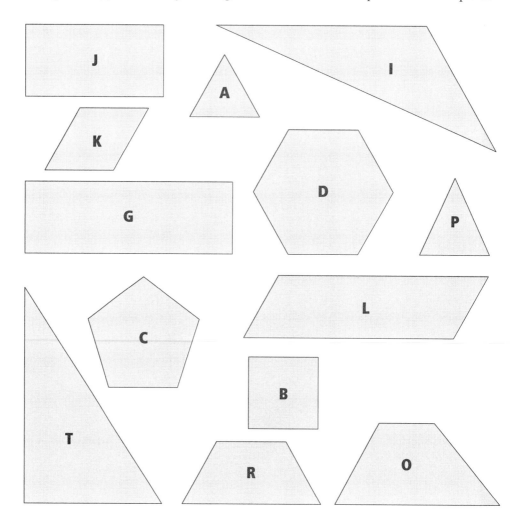

Problem 3.2

Use the shapes shown on page 30 from your ShapeSet™, or cut out copies of the shapes from Labsheet 3.2.

A. Start with four copies of one of the shapes. Try to find a way to put the four copies together—with no overlap and no holes—to make a larger, similar shape. If you are successful, make a sketch showing how the four shapes (rep-tiles) fit together, and give the scale factor from the original shape to

rep-tile to this shape to make the next-largest similar shape. If you are successful, make a sketch showing how the copies fit together. Repeat this process with each rep-tile you found in part A.

Problem 3.2 Follow-Up

1. Examine your work from Problem 3.2 carefully. What is the relationship between the scale factor and the number of copies of an original shape needed to make a larger, similar shape?

2. Is the number of copies of an original shape used to make a new shape related to the side lengths or the area of the new shape?

3.3 Subdividing to Find Rep-tiles

In Problem 3.2, you arranged rep-tiles to form larger, similar shapes. In this problem, you reverse the process. You start with a large shape and try to divide it into smaller, congruent shapes that are similar to the original shape. (Two shapes are *congruent* if they are exactly the same size and shape.) An example is shown at right.

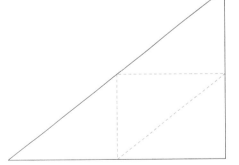

Problem 3.3

The shapes below appear on Labsheet 3.3. Try to find a way to divide each shape into four congruent, smaller shapes that are similar to the original shape. For each shape, give the scale factor from the smaller shape to the original shape.

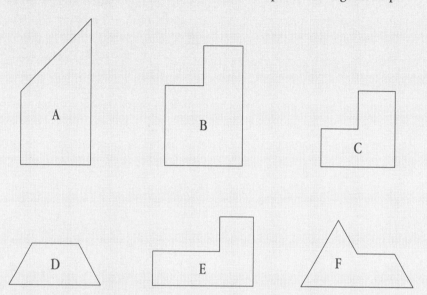

If you have trouble dividing a shape, experiment by cutting out copies of the shape and putting them together as you did in Problem 3.2.

■ Problem 3.3 Follow-Up

1. Choose one of the shapes on Labsheet 3.3. Divide each small figure within the shape in the same way you divided the original shape. How many of these new shapes does it take to cover the original shape?

2. For the shape you subdivided in question 1, what is the scale factor from the smallest shape to the original shape?

3. How does the scale factor from question 2 relate to the number of the smallest shapes it takes to cover the original shape? What is the relationship between the scale factor and the areas of the large and small figures?

As you work on these ACE questions, use your calculator whenever you need it.

Applications

3 cm

1. The sides that form the right angle of a right triangle are

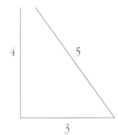

4 5

3

2 a

1.5

a = ?

3.

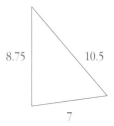

8.75 10.5

7

2.5 b

2

b = ?

4.

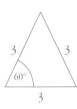

3 3

60°

3

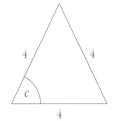

4 4

c

4

c = ?

5.

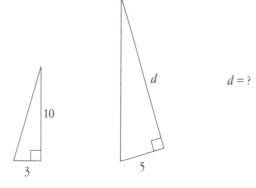

$d = ?$

In 6 and 7, decide which polygon is similar to polygon A. Explain your answer. To check your answer, you may want to trace the figures onto another sheet of paper and cut them out.

6.

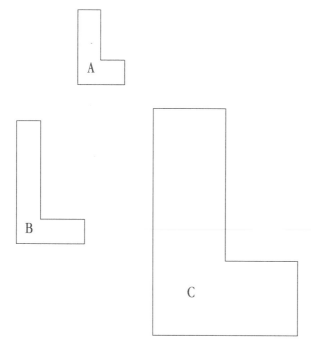

7.

In 8–10, make a copy of the shape. Then, find a way to divide it into four identical, smaller shapes that are each similar to the original shape.

8.

9.

10.

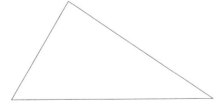

Connections

In 11–14, use this information: The Rosavilla School District wants to build a new middle school building. They asked architects to make scale drawings of some possible layouts for the building. After much discussion, the district narrowed the possibilities to these two:

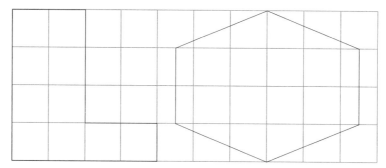

Scale
1 cm = 40 m

11. a. What is the area of the L-shaped scale drawing?

   b. What is the area of the hexagonal scale drawing?

12. a. What would be the area of the L-shaped building?

   b. What would be the area of the hexagonal building?

13. The school board likes the L-shaped layout but wants a building with more space. If they increase the L-shaped model by a scale factor of 2, how would the area of the scale drawing change? How would the area of the building change?

14. After more discussion, the architects made a detailed drawing of the final plans for the building and the school grounds using the scale 1 centimeter = 5 meters.

   a. In the drawing, the fence around the football field is 75 centimeters long. How long will the fence around the actual field be?

   b. In the drawing, the gymnasium floor has an area of $7\frac{1}{2}$ square centimeters. How much floor covering will be needed to build the gym?

c. The music teacher is excited about her new music room! It will be a rectangular room that is 20 meters long and has a floor area of 300 square meters. What are the dimensions of the music room in the scale drawing?

Extensions

15. A **midpoint** is a point that divides a line segment into two equal parts. Each part is one half the length of the original line segment. Draw a figure on grid paper by following these steps:

Step 1 Draw an 8-by-8 square.
Step 2 Mark the midpoint of each side.
Step 3 Connect the midpoints in order with four line segments to form a new figure. (The line segments should not intersect inside the square.)
Step 4 Repeat steps 2 and 3 three more times, each time working with the newest figure.

a. What kind of figure is formed when the midpoints of the sides of a square are connected?

b. Find the area of the original square.

c. Find the area of the new figure that is formed at each step.

d. How do the areas change between successive figures? Look at your drawing. Why does your answer make sense?

e. Are there any similar figures in your drawing? Explain.

16. Rectangle A is similar to rectangle B and also similar to rectangle C. Can you conclude that rectangle B is similar to rectangle C? Explain your answer. Use drawings and examples to illustrate your answer.

17. Are all squares similar? Explain your answer.

18. a. Which shapes below are similar? How do you know?

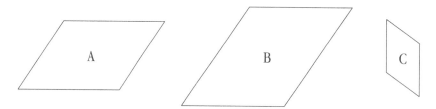

b. State a scale factor for each pair of similar shapes you found in part a. Be specific about the direction of the scale factor. For example, if you found that A and B are similar, state whether the scale factor you give is from A to B or from B to A.

c. For each pair of similar shapes you found, predict how the two areas compare.

19. a. Which shapes below are similar? How do you know?

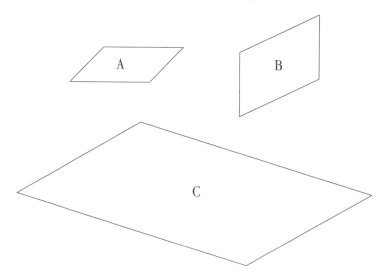

b. State a scale factor for each pair of similar shapes you found in part a. Be specific about the direction of the scale factor. For example, if you found that A and B are similar, state whether the scale factor you give is from A to B or from B to A.

shape?

d. If two shapes are similar, how can you use the scale factor from the smaller shape to the larger shape to predict how the areas of the shapes compare?

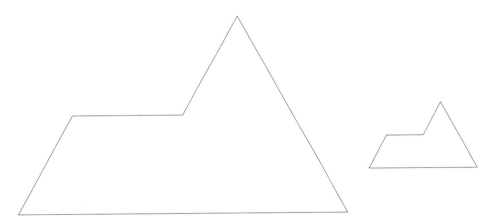

Mathematical Reflections

In this investigation, you determined whether shapes were similar by comparing corresponding parts. You also explored rep-tiles, shapes whose copies can be put together to make larger, similar shapes. These questions will help you summarize what you have learned:

1. How can you decide whether two figures are similar?

2. What does a scale factor between two similar figures tell you?

3. Explain how you can find a scale factor between two similar figures. Use an example to explain your thinking.

4. Explain how you can use the scale factor to determine how the area of an enlarged figure compares to the area of the original figure.

Think about your answers to these questions, discuss your ideas with other students and your teacher, and then write a summary of your findings in your journal.

Using Similarity

By now, you should have a good understanding of what it means for two figures

problems.

4.1 Using Similarity to Solve a Mystery

Many stores, particularly those that stay open late into the night, have surveillance cameras. One night the local Dusk to Dawn convenience store was robbed. The surveillance camera had taken several photographs during the robbery. By inspecting a picture of the robber standing in front of the cash register, police were able to determine the robber's height. How did they do it?

Did you know?

Measurement is used in investigatory and police work all the time. For example, some stores that have surveillance cameras mark a spot on the wall 6 feet from the floor so that, when a person is filmed standing near the wall, it is easier to estimate that person's height. Investigators take measurements of skid marks at the scene of auto accidents to help them determine the speed of the vehicles involved. Photographs and molds may be made of footprints at a crime scene to help determine the type of shoe and the weight of the person who made the prints. And measurements of holes and damage made by bullets can help investigators determine the type of gun that shot the bullet and the direction from which it was shot.

Problem 4.1

The teacher's guides for Connected Mathematics measure $8\frac{1}{2}$" by 11". Below is a photograph of a middle school teacher holding a teacher's guide.

A. Use the photograph to figure out how tall the teacher is. Explain your procedure.

B. How do you think the police determined the robber's height?

Problem 4.1 Follow-Up

1. Estimate the height of the door in the photograph.

2. Do you think your estimate in question 1 is an underestimate or an overestimate? Why?

4.2 Scaling Up

The concept of similarity has many practical applications. For example, designers often make a model of an object and then scale it up or down to make the real object. What kinds of models are likely to be smaller than the real objects? What kinds of models are likely to be larger than the real objects?

Problem 4.2

GOING OUT OF
BUSINESS SALE!
THIS WEEK ONLY!

DISCOUNTS OF 30% to 80%

■ **Problem 4.2 Follow-Up**

What would you suggest Raphael say to the ad department about making a full-page, similar ad from his model?

4.3 Making Copies

When you use a copy machine to enlarge or reduce a document, you are dealing with similarity. On most copy machines, you indicate how much you want to enlarge or reduce something by entering a percent.

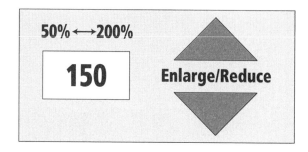

Problem 4.3

Raphael wants to make posters for his sale by enlarging his $8\frac{1}{2}$" by 11" ad. Raphael thinks big posters will get more attention, so he wants to enlarge his ad as much as possible.

The copy machines at the copy shop have cartridges for three paper sizes: $8\frac{1}{2}$" by 11", 11" by 14", and 11" by 17". The machines allow users to enlarge or reduce documents by specifying a percent between 50% and 200%. For example, to enlarge a document by a scale factor of 1.5, a user would enter 150%. This tells the machine to enlarge the document to 150% of its current size.

A. Can Raphael make a poster that is similar to his original ad on any of the three paper sizes—without having to trim off part of the paper? Why or why not?

B. If you were Raphael, what paper size would you use to make a larger, similar poster on the copy machine? What scale factor—expressed as a percent—would you enter into the machine?

■ Problem 4.3 Follow-Up

1. How would you use the copy machines described in the problem to reduce a drawing to 25% of its original size? Remember, the copy machines only accept values between 50% and 200%.

2. How would you use the copy machines to reduce a drawing to $12\frac{1}{2}$% of its original size?

3. How would you use the copy machines to reduce a drawing to 36% of its original size?

4.4 Using Map Scales

We use maps to help us find our way in unfamiliar places, to plan vacations, and to learn about other parts of the world. Maps are like scale drawings: they show a large area of land at a reduced size. To get a sense of the size of the place a map represents, you must know to what scale the map was drawn.

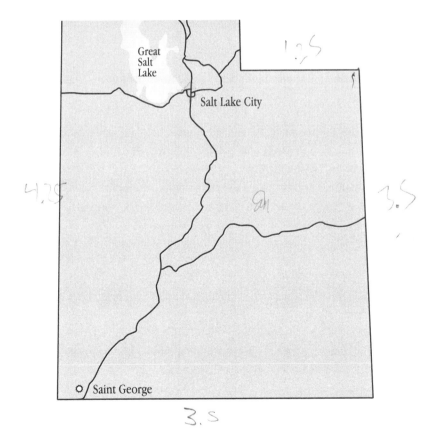

A. How can you use the scale on the map to calculate the scale factor between the map and the real state? What is the scale factor?

B. How many miles of fencing would it take to surround the state of Utah?

C. Use the scale to estimate the area of Utah. Explain your work.

D. If you drove at a steady speed of 55 miles per hour, about how long would it take you to travel from Logan to Saint George?

Problem 4.4 Follow-Up

The total land and water area of the United States is about 3,717,522 square miles. What percent of this total area is the area of Utah?

As you work on these ACE questions, use your calculator whenever you need it.

Applications

1 Find all the pairs of similar rectangles in the set below. For each pair you find, give

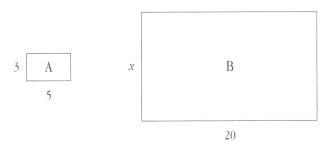

2. The rectangles below are similar.

a. What is the value of *x*?

b. What is the scale factor from rectangle A to rectangle B?

c. Find the area of each rectangle.

d. What is the relationship of the area of rectangle A to the area of rectangle B?

3. The rectangles below are similar.

a. What is the value of x?

b. What is the scale factor from rectangle C to rectangle D?

c. Find the area of each rectangle.

d. What is the relationship of the area of rectangle C to the area of rectangle D?

4. The rectangles below are similar.

a. What is the value of x?

b. What is the scale factor from rectangle E to rectangle F?

c. Find the area of each rectangle.

d. What is the relationship of the area of rectangle E to the area of rectangle F?

5. The rectangles below are similar.

a. What is the value of x?

b. What is the scale factor from rectangle G to rectangle H?

c. Find the area of each rectangle.

d. What is the relationship of the area of rectangle G to the area of rectangle H?

6. Sort the rectangles below into sets of similar rectangles. Describe the method you use.

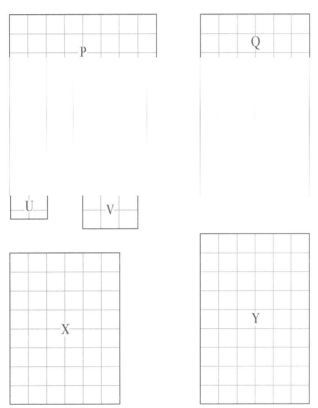

7. Ms. Auito wants to buy new carpeting for her bedroom. The bedroom floor is a rectangle, 9 feet by 12 feet. Carpeting is sold by the square yard.

a. How much carpeting does Ms. Auito need to buy?

b. If the carpeting costs $22 per square yard, how much will the carpet for the bedroom cost?

8. Ms. Auito (from question 7) really liked the carpet she bought for her bedroom, and she would like to buy the same carpet for her large library. The floor of her library is similar to the floor of her 9-foot-by-12-foot bedroom. The scale factor from the bedroom to the library is 2.5.

    a. What are the dimensions of the library?

    b. How much carpeting does Ms. Auito need for the library?

    c. How much will the carpet for the library cost?

9. Here is a drawing of Duke. The scale factor from Duke to the drawing is $12\frac{1}{2}\%$.

    a. How long is Duke from his nose to the tip of his tail?

    b. To build a doghouse for Duke, you would need to know his height so you could make a doorway to accommodate him. How tall is Duke?

    c. The local copy center has a machine that will print on poster-size paper. You can enlarge or reduce a document by specifying a setting between 50% and 200%. How could you use the machine to make a life-size picture of Duke?

10. Samantha drew triangle *ABC* on a grid, then applied a rule to make the triangle on the right.

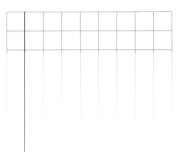 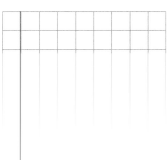

    a. What rule did Samantha apply to make the new triangle?

    b. Is the new triangle similar to triangle *ABC?* Explain. If the triangles are similar, give the scale factor from triangle *ABC* to the new triangle.

11. Samantha drew triangle *JKL* on a grid, then applied a rule to make the triangle on the right.

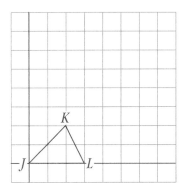 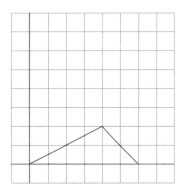

    a. What rule did Samantha apply to make the new triangle?

    b. Is the new triangle similar to triangle *JKL?* Explain. If the triangles are similar, give the scale factor from triangle *JKL* to the new triangle.

12. Samantha drew triangle *XYZ* on a grid, then applied a rule to make the triangle on the right.

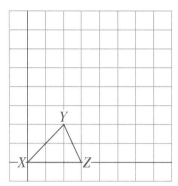 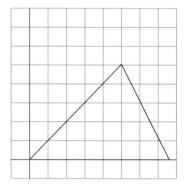

a. What rule did Samantha apply to make the new triangle?

b. Is the new triangle similar to triangle *XYZ?* Explain. If the triangles are similar, give the scale factor from triangle *XYZ* to the new triangle.

13. Examine the figures below.

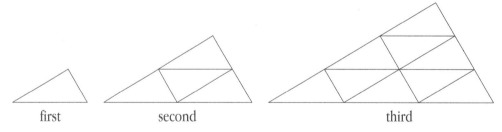

first   second   third

a. If the pattern continues, how many copies of the smallest triangle (the triangle labeled "first") will be in the fourth figure? The fifth figure? The tenth figure? Explain your reasoning.

b. Which of the larger figures is the first figure similar to? For any similar figures you find, give the scale factor from the first figure to the larger figure.

14. A rectangle has a perimeter of 20 centimeters and an area of 24 square centimeters.

    a. Sketch the rectangle on centimeter grid paper.

    b. Find the perimeter and area of the rectangle that is made by enlarging the

15. Rectangles B and C are similar to rectangle A.

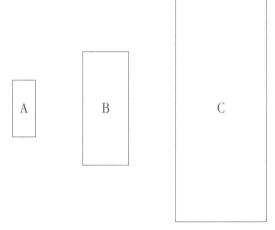

    a. What is the scale factor from rectangle A to rectangle B?

    b. What is the scale factor from rectangle A to rectangle C?

    c. How many rectangle A's would it take to cover rectangle B?

    d. How many rectangle A's would it take to cover rectangle C?

    e. What is the scale factor from rectangle C to rectangle A?

    f. What is the scale factor from rectangle C to rectangle B?

Connections

In 16–19, tell whether the triangles are similar. If they are, give a scale factor.

16.

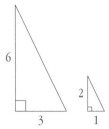

17.

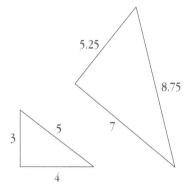

18.

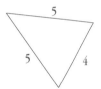

19.

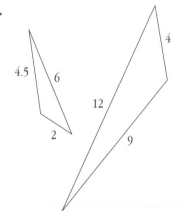

20. a. For each pair of similar triangles in questions 16–19, find the ratio of a side length of the larger triangle to the corresponding side length of the smaller triangle.

   b. How does the ratio of a side length of a larger triangle to the corresponding side length of a smaller, similar triangle relate to the scale factor from the smaller triangle to the larger triangle?

21. On May 3, 1994, Nelson Mandela became the president of South Africa.

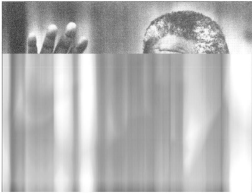

Nelson Mandela

A new flag was created as a symbol of unity. Here is a drawing of the new flag:

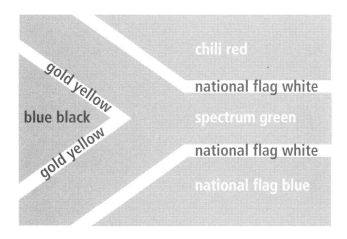

a. What is the area of the blue-black triangle in this drawing? ("Blue-black" is a shade of black.) Take whatever measurements you need to find the area.

b. What is the area of the chili-red section? Explain your reasoning.

c. Estimate the area of the spectrum-green section. Explain your reasoning.

22. Betsine Rosela would like to make a real flag from the drawing in question 21. She has decided that the scale factor from the drawing to her real flag will be 10.

    a. How much blue-black material will Betsine need?

    b. How much chili-red material will she need?

    c. How much spectrum-green material will she need?

    d. How much national-flag-blue material will she need?

23. An antique shop has a large dollhouse that is a model of a real house. The scale factor from the dollhouse to the real house is 12.

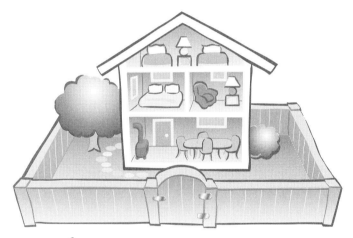

    a. If there is $6\frac{2}{3}$ meters of fencing around the dollhouse, how long is the fence around the real house?

    b. If the area of the living-room floor in the dollhouse is $\frac{1}{4}$ of a square meter, how much carpeting will be needed to cover the living-room floor in the real house?

    c. If it takes $\frac{1}{20}$ of a can of paint to paint the outside of the dollhouse, how many cans would it take to paint the exterior of the real house?

    d. What is the scale factor from the real house to the dollhouse?

    e. If there are four windows on the front of the dollhouse, how many windows are on the front of the real house?

24. On grid paper, draw two triangles that are not similar, if possible. Explain how you know the triangles are not similar. If it is impossible to draw two such triangles, explain why.

25. On grid paper, draw two rectangles that are not similar, if possible. Explain how

corresponding angles, if possible. Explain how you know the rectangles are not similar. If it is impossible to draw two such rectangles, explain why.

28. On grid paper, draw two triangles that are not similar but that have equal corresponding angles, if possible. Explain how you know the triangles are not similar. If it is impossible to draw two such triangles, explain why.

Extensions

29. **a.** Enlarge the drawing of the flag in question 21 by a scale factor of 3. Color your enlarged flag as closely as possible to the indicated colors.

   b. What is the area of the blue-black section in your flag? The chili-red section? The spectrum-green section? Explain how you found your answers.

30. What happens if you enlarge a drawing by a scale factor of 1? Explain your answer. As part of your explanation, draw a picture of a figure and its enlargement by a scale factor of 1.

31. What is the relationship between the areas of two similar figures that are related by a scale factor of 1?

In this investigation, you used scale factors and their relationships to side lengths and areas in similar figures to solve real-world problems. These questions will help you summarize what you have learned:

1 How can you decide whether two figures are similar?

2 What does a scale factor between two similar figures tell you about the relationships between the length and area measures of the figures?

3 If the scale factor from a small figure to a large figure is given as a percent, how can you find the side lengths of the large figure from the side lengths of the small figure?

4 Decide whether each pair of rectangles below is similar. If the rectangles are similar, give the scale factor from the rectangle on the left to the rectangle on the right. If they aren't, explain why.

a.

b.

Think about your answers to these questions, discuss your ideas with other students and your teacher, and then write a summary of your findings in your journal.

Similar Triangles

How tall is your school building? You could find the answer to this question by climbing a ladder and measuring the building with a tape measure, but there

If an object is outdoors, you can use shadows to help estimate its height. The diagram below illustrates how the method works.

On a sunny day, an object casts a shadow. If you hold a meterstick perpendicular to the ground, it will also cast a shadow. The diagram below shows two triangles. One is formed by an object, its shadow, and an imaginary line. The other is formed by a meterstick, its shadow, and an imaginary line. These two triangles are similar.

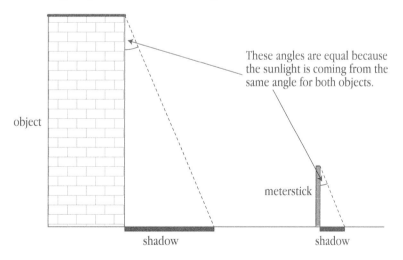

To find the height of the object, you can measure the lengths of the two shadows and apply what you know about similar triangles.

Think about this!

Examine the diagram of the shadow method on the previous page. Can you explain why each angle of the large triangle is equal to the corresponding angle of the small triangle?

Problem 5.1

Mr. Anwar's class is using the shadow method to estimate the height of their school building. They have made the following measurements and sketch:

Length of the meterstick = 1 m
Length of the meterstick's shadow = 0.2 m
Length of the building's shadow = 7 m

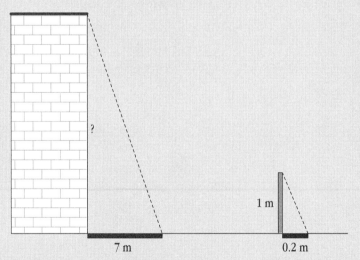

A. Use what you know about similar triangles to find the building's height from the given measurements. Explain your work.

B. With your class, choose a building or other tall object. Work with your group to estimate the object's height using the shadow method. In your answer, include the measurements your group made, and explain in words and drawings how you used these measurements to find the object's height.

Work with your teacher to pool the results from all the groups. Make a line plot of the data. What does your line plot tell you about the object's height? Save the line plot to use in Problem 5.2.

5.2 Using Mirrors to Find Heights

The shadow method is useful for estimating heights, but it only works outdoors and on a sunny day. In this problem, you will use a mirror to help estimate heights. The mirror

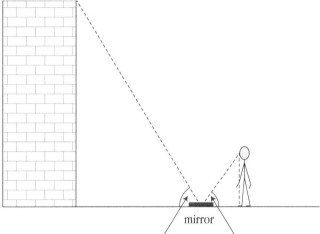

mirror

These angles are equal because light reflects off of a
mirror at the same angle at which it hits the mirror.

To find the object's height, you need to measure three distances and then apply what you know about similar triangles.

Think about this!

Examine the diagram of the mirror method. Can you explain why each angle of the large triangle is equal to the corresponding angle of the small triangle?

Problem 5.2

Jim and Qin-Zhong, students in Mr. Anwar's class, are using the mirror method to estimate the height of their school building. They have made the following measurements and sketch:

Height from the ground to Jim's eyes = 150 cm
Distance from the middle of the mirror to Jim = 100 cm
Distance from the middle of the mirror to the building = 600 cm

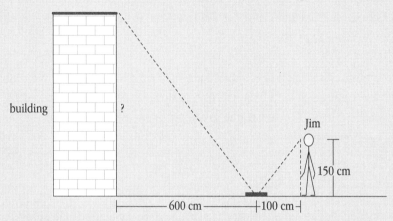

A. Use what you know about similar triangles to find the building's height from the given measurements. Explain your work.

B. With your group, use the mirror method to estimate the height of the same object or building you worked with in Problem 5.1. In your answer, include all the measurements your group made, and explain in words and drawings how you used the measurements to find the object's height.

C. How does the height estimate you made using the shadow method compare with the height estimate you made using the mirror method? Do you think your estimates for the object's height are reasonable? Why or why not?

■ Problem 5.2 Follow-Up

1. Work with your teacher to pool the results from all the groups. Make a line plot of the data.

2. Compare the line plot of the estimates you made using the mirror method to the line plot of the estimates you made using the shadow method (from Problem 5.1 Follow-Up). Which method seems to give more consistent results?

5.3 Using Similar Triangles to Find Distances

Mr. Anwar's class went to Bevort Pond for a picnic. Darnell, Angie, and Trevor wanted to find the distance across the pond. Darnell and Angie suggested that Trevor swim across with the end of a tape measure in his mouth. Trevor declined—the water was very cold! They decided to try to use what they had learned about similar triangles to find the distance across the pond. They drew a diagram and started making the necessary measurements.

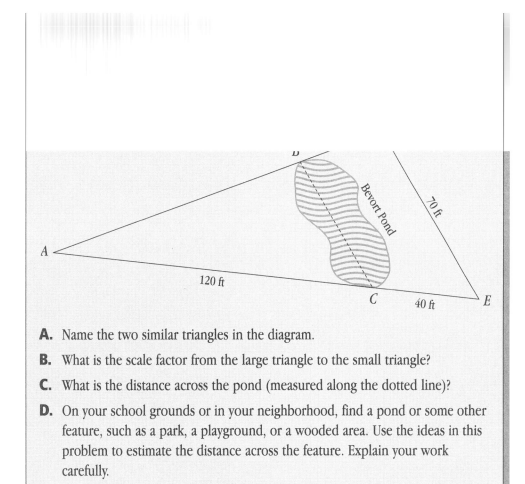

A. Name the two similar triangles in the diagram.

B. What is the scale factor from the large triangle to the small triangle?

C. What is the distance across the pond (measured along the dotted line)?

D. On your school grounds or in your neighborhood, find a pond or some other feature, such as a park, a playground, or a wooded area. Use the ideas in this problem to estimate the distance across the feature. Explain your work carefully.

■ Problem 5.3 Follow-Up

Is the large triangle Darnell, Angie, and Trevor measured the only one that will work to find the distance across the pond? If you think other triangles could be used, make a drawing of Bevort Pond showing another triangle that could be measured to determine the distance across the pond. If you think no other triangles would work, explain why not.

As you work on these ACE questions, use your calculator whenever you need it.

Applications

1. The triangles below are similar.

    a. Name all pairs of corresponding sides.

    b. Name all pairs of corresponding angles.

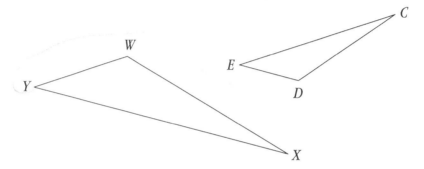

2. **a.** In the figure below, identify the similar triangles.

    b. Name all pairs of corresponding sides for the similar triangles you found.

    c. Name all pairs of corresponding angles for the similar triangles you found.

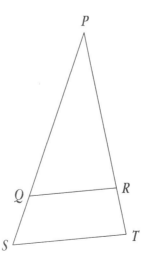

3. Daphne used the shadow method to estimate the height of the basketball backboard on the school playground. Here are the measurements she recorded. Use them to find the distance from the ground to the top of the backboard.

Length of meterstick = 1 m   Length of meterstick's shadow = $\frac{1}{2}$ m

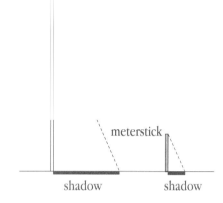

4. Darius used the shadow method to estimate the height of the flagpole in front of the city library. Here are the measurements he recorded. Use them to find the height of the flagpole.

Length of meterstick = 1 m   Length of meterstick's shadow = 5 cm
Length of flagpole's shadow = 38 cm

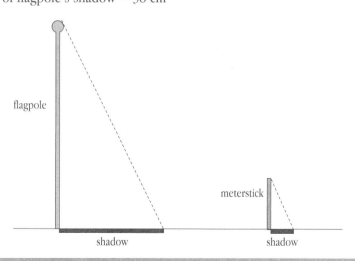

5. The principal asked Hank to demonstrate what he was learning in math class. Hank decided to use the mirror method to estimate the principal's height. Here are the measurements Hank recorded. Use them to find the principal's height.

Height from the ground to Hank's eyes = 1.5 m
Distance from the center of the mirror to Hank = 3 m
Distance from the center of the mirror to the principal = 3.7 m

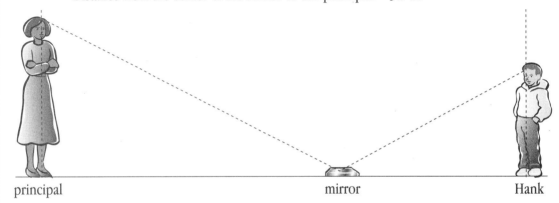

principal   mirror   Hank

6. Stacia and Byron used the mirror method to estimate the height of their math classroom. Below are the measurements and sketch they made. Use them to find the height of the classroom.

Height from the ground to Stacia's eyes = 1.5 m
Distance from the center of the mirror to Stacia = 1 m
Distance from the center of the mirror to the classroom wall = 2.4 m

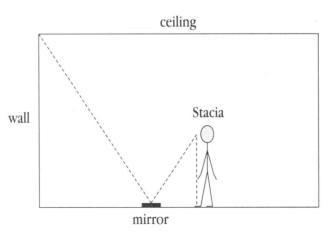

ceiling

wall   Stacia

mirror

7. A stick 2 meters long casts a shadow 0.5 meters long. At the same time, the Washington Monument casts a shadow 42.25 meters long. How tall is the Washington Monument?

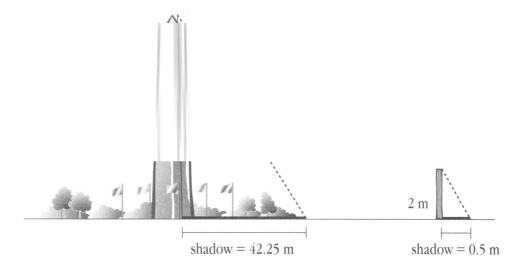

shadow = 42.25 m   2 m   shadow = 0.5 m

8. Joan used a mirror to estimate the height of a flagpole. Below are the measurements she recorded. What is the height of the flagpole?

Height from the ground to Joan's eyes = 5 feet
Distance from the center of the mirror to Joan = 2 feet
Distance from the center of the mirror to the flagpole = 9 feet

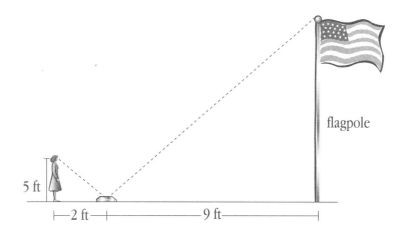

flagpole

5 ft

|—2 ft—|————9 ft————|

9. What is the distance across the gravel pit shown in the drawing?

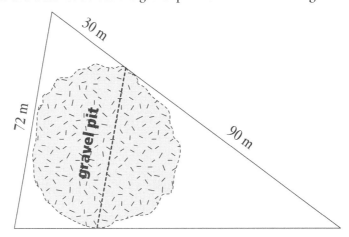

Connections

10. Look carefully at the figure below.

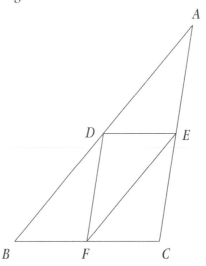

a. Which line segments look parallel?

b. Segment *DE* connects the midpoints of segments *AB* and *AC*. How does the length of segment *BC* compare to the length of segment *DE?* Explain.

11. Look carefully at the figure below.

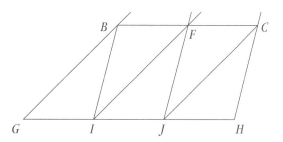

a. Which line segments look parallel?

b. How does this figure relate to the figure in question 10?

c. How does the length of segment *DE* compare to the length of segment *BC* and segment *GH?*

d. How are line segments *CJ*, *EI*, and *AG* related?

e. How are line segments *BI*, *DJ*, and *AH* related?

Extensions

12. Use the mirror method, the shadow method, or another method involving similar triangles to find the height of a telephone pole, a light pole, or a statue in your town. Report your results, and explain your method.

13. Tang plans to make some repairs on the roof of a building. He needs a ladder to reach the roof, but he's not sure how long the ladder should be. He thinks he has found a way to use similar triangles to find the height of the building. He stands 9 meters from the building and holds a 30-centimeter ruler in front of his eyes. The ruler is 45 centimeters from his eyes. He can just see the top and bottom of the building as he looks above and below the ruler.

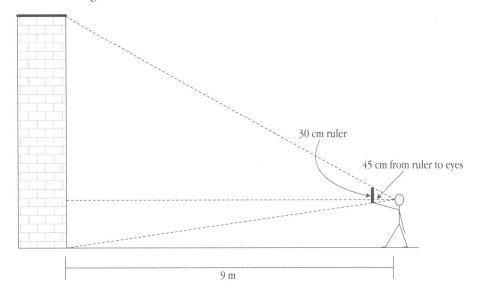

30 cm ruler

45 cm from ruler to eyes

9 m

a. Do you see any similar triangles in the diagram that can help Tang figure out how tall the building is? Explain.

b. How tall is the building? Explain your reasoning.

14. In an *annular eclipse,* the Moon moves between the Earth and Sun, blocking part of the Sun's light for a few minutes. The Moon does not entirely cover the Sun; instead, a ring of light appears around the shadow of the Moon. In about 240 B.C., Aristarchus used eclipses to help correctly calculate the distances between the Earth, Moon, and Sun.

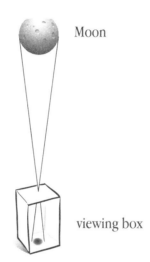

Moon

viewing box

During the eclipse, the image of the Moon almost completely covered the Sun. The Moon's shadow and the ring of light surrounding it appeared on the bottom of the viewing box. The Moon's image was 1 meter from the hole and had a diameter of 0.9 centimeter. The class read in their science book that the actual diameter of the Moon is about 3500 kilometers. Use this data to find the distance to the Moon at the time of the eclipse.

15. **a.** Some evening when you see a full moon, go outside with a friend and use a coin to exactly block the image of the moon. How far from your eyes do you have to hold the coin? Can you hold the coin yourself, or does your friend have to hold it for you?

b. The diameter of the Moon is about 2160 miles, and the distance from the Earth to the Moon is about 238,000 miles. Use these numbers, the diameter of your coin, and the concept of similar triangles to compute the distance you would have to hold the coin from your eye to just block the Moon. How does the distance you computed compare to the distance you measured in your experiment?

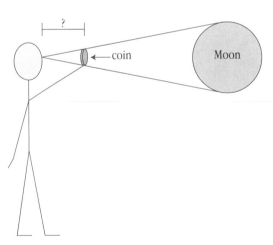

16. Parallel lines *BD* and *EG* below are cut by line *AH*. Eight angles are formed by the lines—four around point *C* and four around point *F*.

a. Find every angle that appears to be congruent to ∠*ACD*.

b. Find every angle that appears to be congruent to ∠*EFC*.

Mathematical Reflections

In this investigation, you used what you know about similar triangles to find heights of buildings and to estimate other inaccessible distances. These questions will help you summarize what you have learned:

1. Explain at least two ways you can use similar triangles to measure things in the real world. Illustrate your ideas with an example.

2. What properties of similar triangles are useful for estimating distances and heights?

3. If you take any two similar triangles and place the small triangle on top of the large triangle so that a pair of corresponding angles match, what can you say about the sides of the two triangles opposite these corresponding angles?

Think about your answers to these questions, discuss your ideas with other students and your teacher, and then write a summary of your findings in your journal.

INVESTIGATION 6

Stretching and Shrinking with

6.1 Drawing Similar Figures with a Computer

The problems in this investigation use only two commands: fd (forward) and rt (right turn).

When you begin a new *Turtle Math* session, you will see a turtle facing upward in the center of the Drawing window.

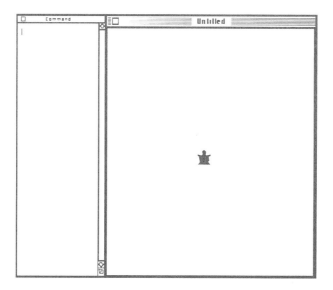

You tell the turtle how to move by typing commands in the Command window. Try telling the turtle to move forward: type fd, followed by a space, followed by a number. The number tells the turtle how many steps to take.

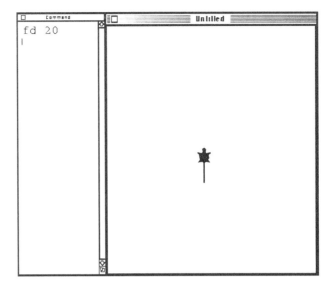

As the turtle moves, it leaves a track on the screen. Type another fd command to make the turtle go farther.

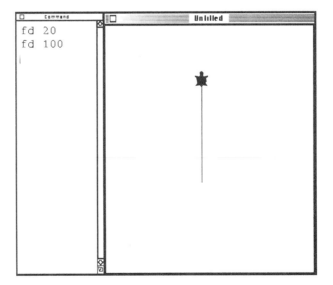

Now try making the turtle change direction: type the `rt` command, followed by a space, followed by a number. The number tells the turtle how many degrees to the right (clockwise) to turn.

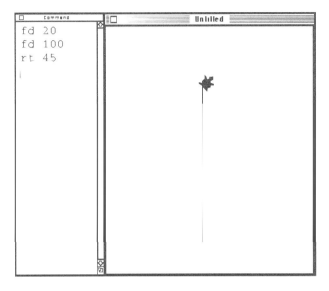

Notice that the turtle does not leave a track when you type a `rt` command. The `rt` command only tells the turtle to face a new direction. To continue drawing the track, type another `fd` command.

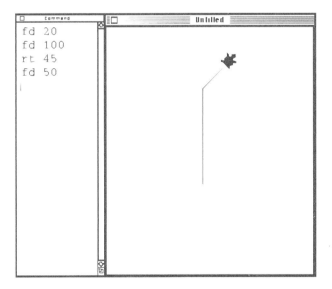

A selection of tools appears at the top of the *Turtle Math* screen. In this problem, you will use the Scale tool and the Change Shape tool. These tools let you change the size and shape of a figure.

Scale

Change Shape

Problem 6.1

Choose one of the figures below. Make the figure by typing the commands in the Command window.

Equilateral triangle	Rectangle	Right trapezoid
fd 60	fd 30	fd 52
rt 120	rt 90	rt 90
fd 60	fd 70	fd 30
rt 120	rt 90	rt 60
fd 60	fd 30	fd 60
	rt 90	rt 120
	fd 70	fd 60

After you've drawn the figure, save a copy of it on your computer. To save the drawing, select Save My Work from the File menu. Type a name for your drawing and then click on Save. After you've saved a copy of your drawing, experiment with using the Scale tool and Change Shape tool on your figure. Anytime you want to return to the original figure, just choose Open My Work from the File menu and select the name you chose for your drawing.

A. Which features of the original figure change when you use the Scale tool? Which features of the original figure change when you use the Change Shape tool? Be sure to discuss numbers of sides, side lengths, and angle measures.

B. Which features of the original figure stay the same when you use the Scale tool? Which features of the original figure stay the same when you use the Change Shape tool?

■ Problem 6.1 Follow-Up

Can either of the tools you investigated be used to create similar figures? To justify your answer, make sketches of what you see on the computer screen including side lengths and angle measures.

6.2 Stretching and Shrinking Flags

You have already studied how scale factors are related to lengths and areas of similar figures. *Turtle Math* is an excellent tool for investigating this concept further.

Problem 6.2

The set of commands below will draw a flag. Type in the commands exactly as they are shown; don't use any shortcuts. When you are finished, save a copy of

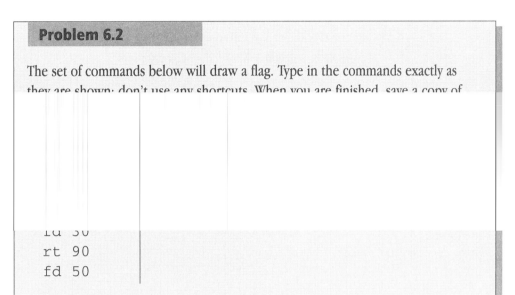

```
ld 50
rt 90
fd 50
```

Use the Scale tool to make enlargements and reductions of the flag. Make a chart like the one below, and fill in the missing information.

Scale factor	Sketch of figure	Height of flagpole	Length of flag	Width of flag	Area of flag
1	50 ▯ 30 / 80	80 steps	50 steps	30 steps	1500 square steps
2					
0.5					
−1					

■ Problem 6.2 Follow-Up

1. What happens to the flag when it is changed by a negative scale factor? Explain why you think this happens.

2. Which scale factors make a flag that is the same size as the original?

3. Which scale factors make a flag that is smaller than the original?

4. Which scale factors make a flag that is larger than the original?

As you work on these ACE questions, use your calculator whenever you need it.

Applications

```
rt 144
fd 80
rt 144
fd 80
```

a. Change Tonya's program to draw a star that is similar to Tonya's but a different size.

b. What is the scale factor from Tonya's star to the star your program draws?

Connections

2. Squares A and B were made using *Turtle Math.* The Grid tool was used to display a coordinate grid. You can use the grid to measure the size of each square in numbers of turtle steps.

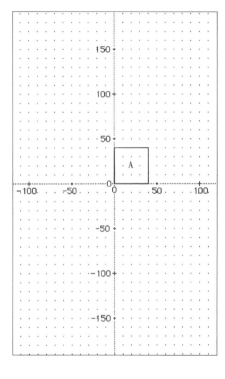 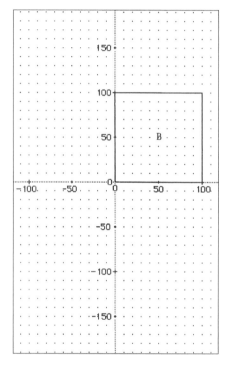

a. What is the scale factor from square A to square B?

b. What is the scale factor from square B to square A?

Extensions

3. The drawing below shows the Drawing window, with a grid, before any commands are entered.

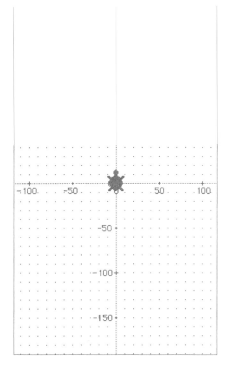

a. Jeff entered the commands below. Make a sketch that shows the turtle's new position.

```
fd  -20
fd  -35
fd  15
fd  -70
fd  160
```

b. Jeff erased the commands to return the turtle to its starting point. Then, he entered each command *twice*. Make a sketch that shows the turtle's new position.

Mathematical Reflections

In this unit, you have explored what the word *similar* means in mathematics. These questions will help you summarize what you have learned:

1 If two figures are similar, what characteristics of the figures are the same?

2 If two figures are similar, what characteristics of the figures may be different?

3 What does a scale factor tell you about two similar figures?

Think about your answers to these questions, discuss your ideas with other students and your teacher, and then write a summary of your findings in your journal.

All-Similar Shapes

A group of students decided to look at rectangles that are square. They found that no matter what size square they drew, every square was similar to shape B in the ShapeSet and to all other squares. They concluded that *all squares are similar!* They decided to call a square an All-Similar shape.

The students wondered whether there were any other All-Similar shapes like the square. That is, are there any other groups of shapes called by the same name that are similar to all other shapes called by that name? Use your ShapeSet to investigate this question.

1. Make a list of the names of all the different types of shapes in the ShapeSet—squares, rectangles, triangles, equilateral triangles, circles, and regular hexagons.

2. For each type of shape, list the shapes (using their letter names) that belong in that group.

3. Sort the different types of shapes into two groups: All-Similar shapes (such as squares) and shapes that are not All-Similar (such as rectangles).

4. Describe the ways in which All-Similar shapes are alike.

Unit Reflections

Working on the problems in this unit helped you to understand the concept of *similarity* as it is applied to geometric shapes. You learned how to create similar shapes and how to determine whether two shapes are similar. You also discovered the relationships between the areas and perimeters of similar shapes and investigated applications using properties of similar shapes.

Using Your Understanding of Similarity—To test your understanding of similarity consider the following problems that ask you to recognize similar shapes and deduce their properties.

1 *The square has been subdivided into six triangles and four parallelograms. Some pairs of triangles and some pairs of parallelograms are similar.*

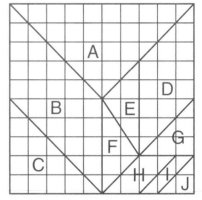

a. List two pairs of similar triangles in the figure. For each pair, give a scale factor that describes the size relationship of the two triangles.

b. Pick one pair of similar triangles and explain how their perimeters are related and how their areas are related.

c. List several pairs of triangles in the figure that are *not similar.*

d. List all pairs of similar parallelograms in the figure. For each pair, give a scale factor that describes the size relationship between the two parallelograms.

e. Pick two similar parallelograms and explain how their perimeters are related and how their areas are related.

f. List several pairs of parallelograms in the figure that are *not similar.*

2 *Suppose that a triangle is drawn on a coordinate grid.*

a. Which of the following rules will transform the given triangle into a similar triangle?

    i. $(3x, 3y)$ **ii.** $(x + 3, y + 2)$ **iii.** $(2x, 4x)$

    iv. $(2x, 2y + 1)$ **v.** $(1.5x, 1.5y)$

b. For each of the rules in part a that will produce a shape similar to the original triangle, give the scale factor from the original triangle to its image.

gave by applying those basic principles of similarity.

1. What condition(s) must be satisfied for two polygons to be called similar? What questions do you ask yourself when deciding whether two shapes are similar?

2. Suppose shape A is similar to shape B and the scale factor from A to B is a number k.

    a. How will the perimeters of the two figures be related?

    b. How will the areas of the two figures be related?

3. If two triangles are similar, what do you know about

    a. the measures of sides in the two figures?

    b. the measures of angles in the two figures?

4. Which of the following statements about similarity are true and which are false?

    a. Any two equilateral triangles are similar.

    b. Any two rectangles are similar.

    c. Any two squares are similar.

    d. Any two isosceles triangles are similar.

You will study and use ideas of similarity in several future *Connected Mathematics* units, especially when it is important to compare sizes and shapes of geometric figures. Basic principles of similarity are also used in a variety of practical and scientific problems when enlarging or shrinking of images is needed as in photography and photocopying.

compare When we compare objects, we examine them to determine how they are alike and how they are different. We compare when we classify objects by size, color, weight, or shape. We compare when we decide that two figures have the same shape or that they are not similar.

congruent figures Figures that have corresponding angles of the same measure and corresponding sides of the same length.

coordinate graphing Making a graph using pairs of numbers (x, y)—called the x- and y-coordinates—to locate positions on a coordinate plane. The x-coordinate tells how far to move right or left (horizontally) from the origin, and the y-coordinate tells how far to move up or down (vertically). The combination of the two moves locates a unique point in the plane. For example, the pair of numbers $(3, {}^-0.5)$ indicates the point 3 units to the right of the origin and 0.5 units down.

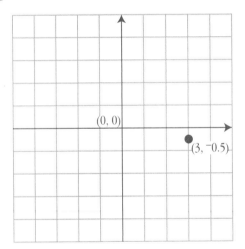

corresponding Corresponding sides or angles have the same relative position in similar figures. In this pair of similar shapes, side *AB* corresponds to side *A′B′*, and ∠*BCD* corresponds to ∠*B′C′D′*.

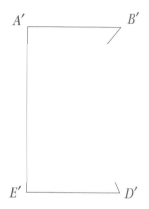

image The figure that results from some transformation of a figure. It is often of interest to consider what is the same and what is different between a figure and its image.

ratio A ratio is a comparison of two quantities that tells the scale between them. Here are some examples of uses of ratios:

- In the similar figures above, suppose *AB* = 2 and *A′B′* = 3. Then the ratio of the length of *AB* to the length of *A′B′* is $\frac{2}{3}$. The ratio of the length of *A′B′* to the length of *AB* is $\frac{3}{2}$.

- If a small figure is enlarged by a scale factor of 2, the ratio of the small figure's area to the large figure's area will be $\frac{1}{4}$. The ratio of the large figure's area to the small figure's area will be $\frac{4}{1}$ or 4.

scale factor The number used to multiply the coordinates of a figure to stretch or shrink it. If the scale factor is 3, all the lengths in the image are three times the corresponding lengths in the original. If the scale factor is $\frac{2}{3}$, the image has lengths $\frac{2}{3}$ those of the original. The scale factor can be found by forming the ratio, or quotient, of the length of a side of the image to the length of the corresponding side in the original. The scale factor can be given as a fraction, a decimal, or a percent. If the scale factor is larger than 1, the image is larger than the original figure. If the scale factor is positive but less than 1, the image is smaller than the original figure. If the scale factor is 1, the original and the image are congruent. On a coordinate grid, it can be seen that scale factors less than 0 flip the figure over the x and y axes in addition to stretching or shrinking it. Scale factors between 0 and $^-1$ shrink the original; scale factors less than $^-1$ stretch the original, and a scale factor of $^-1$ produces an image congruent to the original but at a different place in the plane.

similar figures Figures with the same shape. Two figures are mathematically similar if and only if their corresponding angles are equal and the ratios of all pairs of corresponding sides are equal. The ratio $\dfrac{\text{image side length}}{\text{original side length}}$ is the scale by which all sides of the original figure "stretch" or "shrink" into the corresponding sides of the image figure.

Index